Do I Need a Car?

by Mrs. Siegel's class
with Tony Stead

capstone

Wants and Needs

by Miguel

We told our teacher, "We need new classroom toys!" But do we really need toys? We already have construction blocks, modeling clay, and lots of board games. We want new classroom toys, but we don't really need new toys.

What are wants? What are needs? How are wants and needs different? Read this book to learn more about wants and needs.

What Are Needs?

by Lahari and Vyshnavi

Needs are things we have to have in order to survive. We need certain things in order to stay healthy and safe.

Things we need:

- We need shelter to keep us warm and protect us from bad weather.
- We need clothing to keep ourselves warm and protect our skin from the sun.
- We need fresh, clean water to keep our bodies healthy and hydrated.
- We all need clean air to breathe.
- We need sleep to keep us healthy.
- We need healthy food to help our bodies grow and provide us with energy.

clean air
shelter
Needs
clean water
clothing
healthy foods

Last but not least, all people need to be loved and cared for. We need people to take care of us and help us get the other things we need to survive. We can't see love and care but we still need them.

illustrated by Ethan and Tanush

What Are Wants?

by Christina, Deakon, Ethan, Marcello, and Tanush

Wants are things that we do not need in order to survive. For example, you might think you need a tall, cold, and refreshing glass of lemonade but what you really need is a tall, cold, and refreshing glass of water. You want the lemonade but you do not need it to survive. Our bodies need to stay hydrated with water.

Another example could be a donut. Say you were hungry and you were thinking of a donut. But what you really need is a nutritious, healthful snack like an apple. The apple will keep your body healthy and strong. The donut is just filled with sugar and fat. That's not what your body needs to stay healthy and energized.

Want
Need
unhealthy
healthy
?

Examples of Wants

Some examples of wants would be toys, candy, and electronics. These are all items that we do not need but may REALLY want!

Another example of a want is toys. Toys are nice to have but do you need a toy to survive? Of course, the answer is "NO"! Wants are things that we like to have but do not need in order to survive.

Wants
candy
Electronics
Roller skates
pets
Pop
toys
remote control car
23
skate board
cool shoes

How Can You Tell Wants and Needs Apart?

By David, Ethan, and Izzy

Sometimes it's hard to tell what is a want and what is a need. You might think you need a cool, fancy backpack that costs more money than a basic backpack. The truth is, you don't need a cool, fancy backpack. All you really need is a basic bag to hold your supplies.

Suppose you wanted a new toy but what you really need is a new pair of shoes. Your old shoes are too small and way too tight!

You decide to buy the shoes because they are needed to protect your feet. If you have any money left over you can buy what you want, like that new toy.

illustrated by Christina and Lahari

People usually buy the things they need first, and if they have money left over, they can buy the things they want.

Do I Really Need a Car?

A car can be a need or a want. A person may feel like he or she needs a car to travel from one place to another. However, there are other ways to travel. For example, a person can walk, use a bike, ride a bus, or use another type of transportation.

Maybe you live where there are no buses or trains. Perhaps you need to get somewhere that is too far away for walking or cycling. So you really do need a car. But that doesn't mean you need a really big, fancy, or fast car. You just need a car that is safe and can get you from one place to another.

Needs are things you have to have, and wants are things you would like to have!

Wants	Needs